THE STORY OF JANE GOODALL

A Biography Book for New Readers

Written by
SUSAN B. KATZ

Illustrated by
LINDSAY DALE SCOTT

ROCKRIDGE PRESS

To the late Dr. William (Bill) Stapp, my mentor and professor of environmental education at the University of Michigan. Also, in memory of the late Ilse Abshagen Leitinger and Ann-Marie Parsons, and to all of the people, like Luis Hernan Solano, still protecting La Cangreja, the Costa Rican rain forest we worked to convert into a national park.

For general information on our other products and services or to obtain technical support, please contact our Customer Care Department within the United States at (866) 744-2665, or outside the United States at (510) 253-0500.

Rockridge Press publishes its books in a variety of electronic and print formats. Some content that appears in print may not be available in electronic books, and vice versa.

Series Designer: Angela Navarra
Interior and Cover Designer: Jane Archer
Art Producer: Hillary Frileck
Editor: Orli Zuravicky
Production Manager: Jose Olivera
Production Editor: Nora Milman

Illustrations © 2020 Lindsay Dale Scott; Creative Market/Semicircular, pp. 3, 10, 13, 27, 34, 37; Shutterstock/Tinseltown, p. 45; Alamy Stock Photo/Danita Delimont, p. 47; Getty Images/Popperfoto, p. 48. Author photo courtesy of Jeanne Marquis

ISBN: Print 978-1-64611-873-1 | eBook 978-1-64611-874-8

R1

Printed in China

CONTENTS

CHAPTER 1

A SCIENTIST IS BORN

Meet Jane Goodall

Jane Goodall was born with a love of nature, especially animals. When she was just one and a half, Jane took a handful of earthworms to bed with her. As soon as Jane's mom explained that worms need soil to live, Jane ran outside and returned the worms to their garden.

Jane's dad also saw her love of animals. He bought her a stuffed chimpanzee named Jubilee. Jane loved Jubilee and took him nearly everywhere she went. Today, all these years later, she still keeps Jubilee with her.

Jane grew up to be one of the most important **naturalists** in the world. She loved animals so much that she didn't just study them; Jane helped save them, too. When she learned that chimpanzees were losing their **habitat**, or home, in Africa, Jane had to do something. Helping save the chimps became Jane's life purpose and passion.

JUMP IN THE THINK TANK

Why is it important for people to speak up for and save animals and their habitats?

> "What you do makes a difference and you must decide what kind of a difference you want to make."

Jane has worked for 60 years to save the chimpanzees from **extinction**, or disappearing. Let's find out how Jane went from being a little girl who loved animals to becoming an important scientist who led the longest wildlife **conservation** effort in history!

David Greybeard

Flo

Fifi

Freud

Mr. McGregor

Flint

Jane's England

Valerie Jane Morris-Goodall was born in London, England, on April 3, 1934. Her younger sister, Judy, was born on Jane's fourth birthday. When Jane was five, her family moved to France. Jane's parents, Mortimer and Vanne, wanted the girls to learn French. After just a few months, World War II broke out, and it was no longer safe to stay in France.

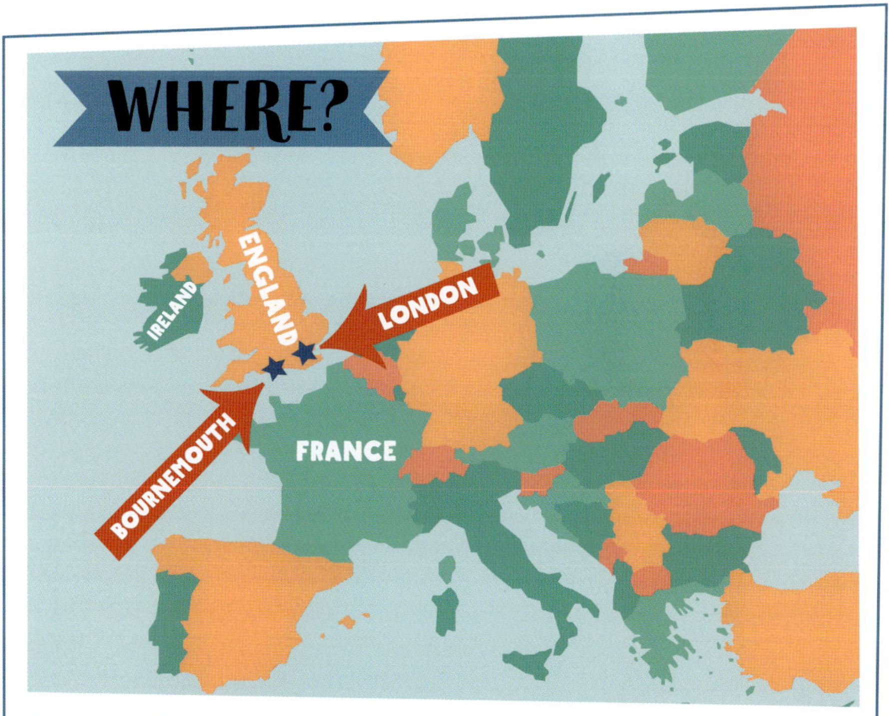

When they returned to England, the family moved to where Jane's dad had grown up. There was an ancient castle on the grounds. Jane loved to explore it with Judy, although sometimes it seemed scary to them with its big spiderwebs and bats!

Shortly after they moved, Jane's dad left to join the British Army. Jane, her mother, and Judy

went to live with Jane's grandmother in the seaside English town of Bournemouth.

It was a beautiful place. Jane would often go horseback riding, walk along the beach, or wander in the forest. She was very **observant** and loved watching animals. One special tree became her favorite place to read. Little did Jane know that her love of nature would take her from backyard adventures to becoming a champion for chimpanzees.

WHEN?

Jane is born in London, England.

APRIL 3,

1934

Jane's sister, Judy, is born. Jane turns 4.

1938

Jane's family moves to France. World War II begins.

1939

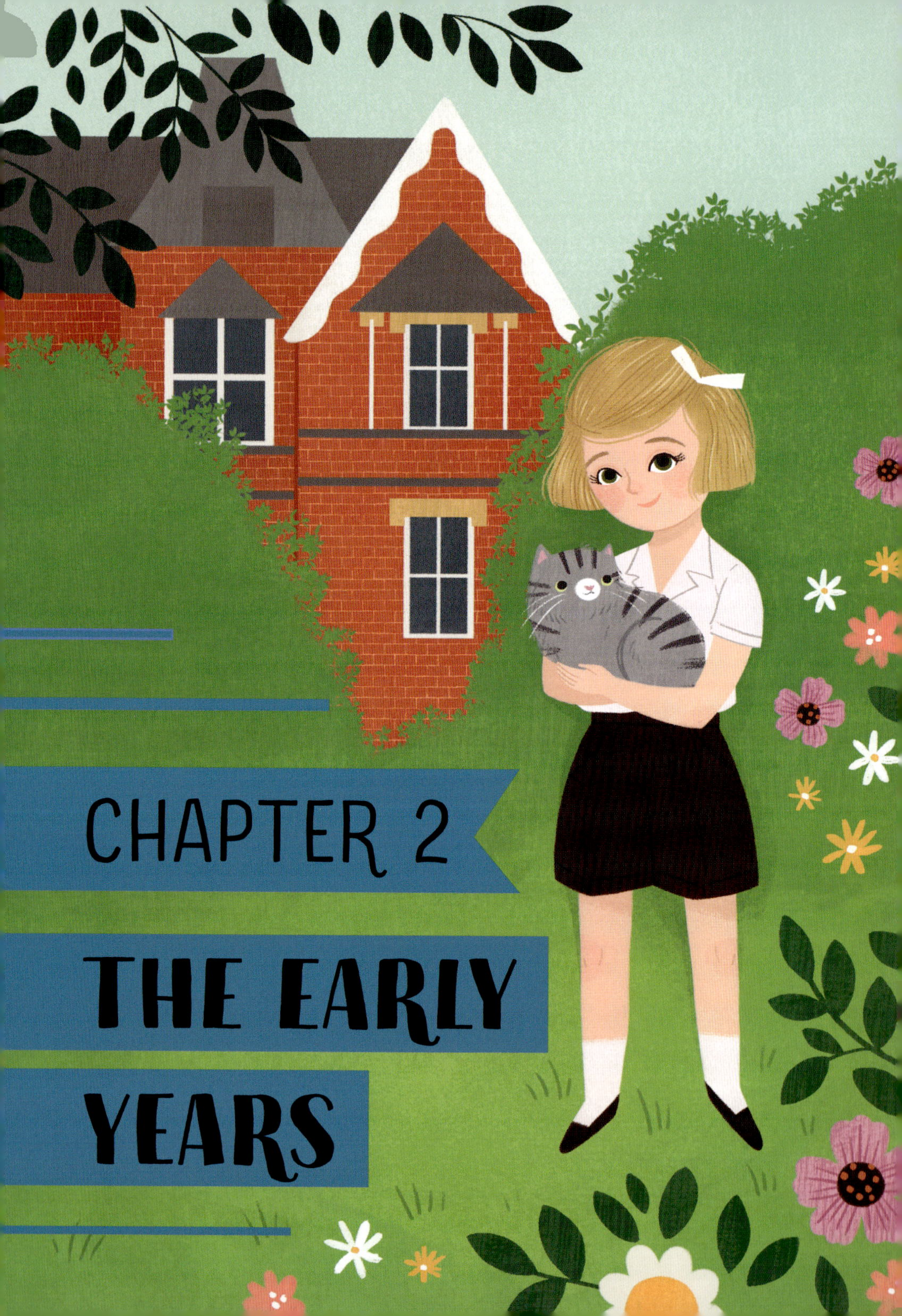

CHAPTER 2

THE EARLY YEARS

Animals' Best Friend

Jane loved living near the sea. Once in a while, her mother would take Jane and her sister to a relative's farm in the country. Curious, four-year-old Jane wanted to understand how hens lay eggs. So Jane sat in the hen cage and waited. Hours later, the hen came in and settled down. Jane watched and waited. Finally, the hen wiggled out an egg. Jane gasped with excitement. This was her first real animal observation. Jane ran home to tell her mother all about it.

Jane's mother took her to the library often. There, she found a book called *The Story of Doctor Dolittle* by Hugh Lofting. Jane loved how Dr. Doolittle spoke to the animals so much that she read it over and over again.

Then, Jane discovered *The Jungle Book* and the Tarzan series. The only thing Tarzan did wrong, in Jane's eyes, was marry the wrong Jane! At age eight, inspired by Tarzan, Jane began to dream of working with animals in Africa.

Jane loved to watch the wild animals near her house. So, she started a nature group

Goodall Family Tree

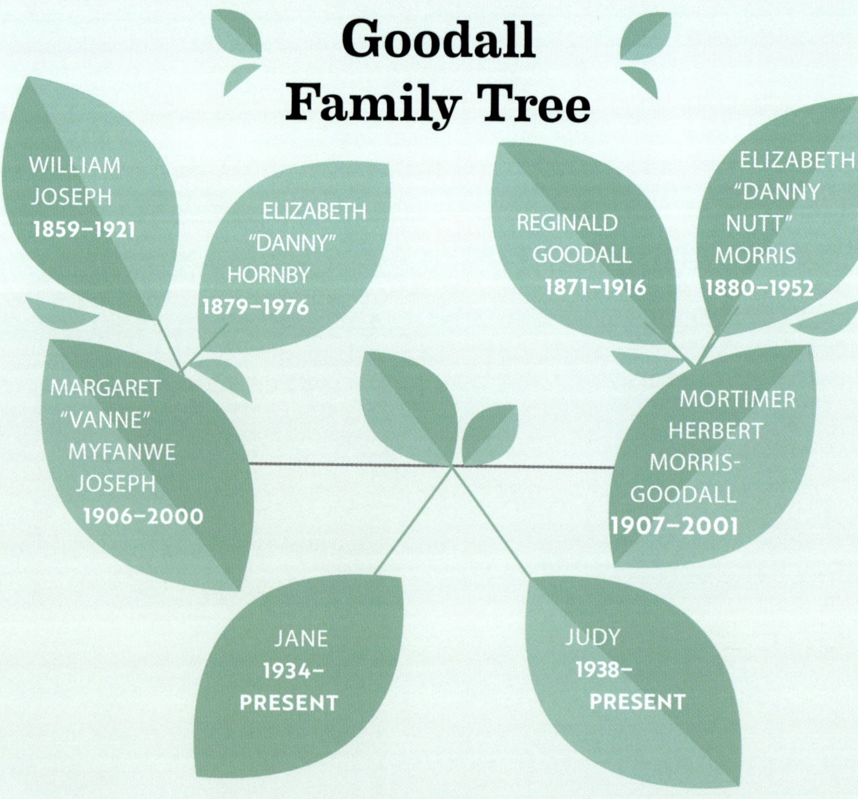

called the Alligator Club with her sister and two neighborhood girls. They even published *The Alligator Magazine* with all of their notes about animals!

MYTH & FACT

MYTH: Her stuffed animal Jubilee is the reason Jane ended up studying chimpanzees.

FACT: Dr. Louis Leakey, a leading scientist, chose chimps as the animal Jane would work with in Africa.

Dreams of Africa

Jane enjoyed learning about biology, the study of living things, in school. She was very bright and was usually at the top of her class. Still, when Jane graduated from high school, there weren't many job options for women. Jane's mother suggested that she go to school in London to become a secretary, so she did.

But Jane thought being a secretary was boring. She couldn't stop thinking about her dream of traveling to Africa to study animals. Then, one day, Jane got a letter from an old school friend named Clo. She wanted Jane to visit her in Kenya. First, Jane needed to earn the money for her ticket.

Jane quit her job as a secretary and moved back home to save money. She became a waitress. After about five months of hard work, Jane had saved enough for a ticket to Africa! Her dream was coming true.

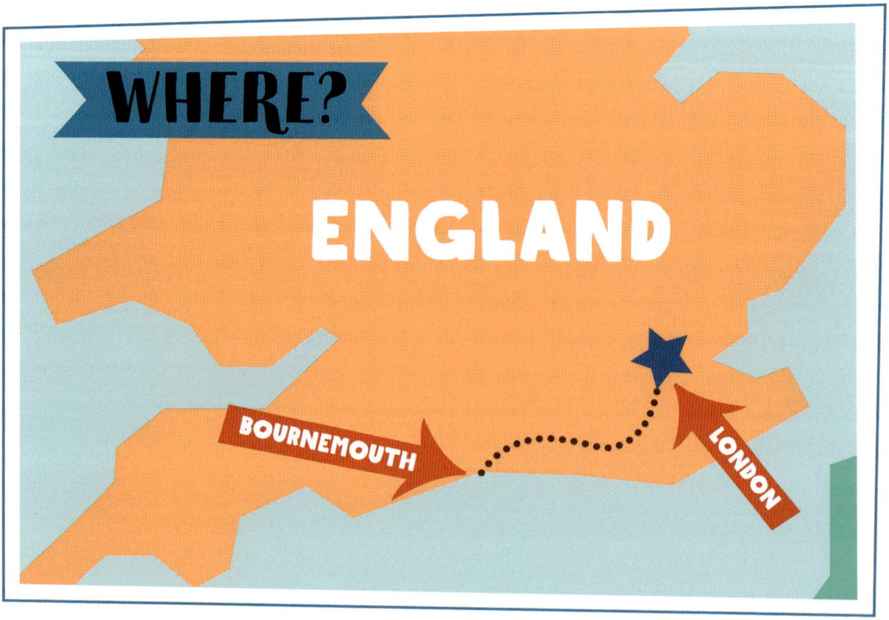

JUMP IN THE THINK TANK

How does staying focused help you reach a goal? Do you have a goal that you want to reach someday? If so, what is it?

WHEN?

Jane graduates from high school.	Jane starts secretarial school.	Clo invites Jane to Kenya, Africa.
1952	**1953**	**1956**

CHAPTER 3

OFF TO AFRICA!

Adventure Calls

On March 13, 1957, Jane boarded a ship called the *Kenya Castle* that was sailing to Africa. After a three-week-long journey, Jane arrived in Kenya. Then, she began a two-day train ride to Nairobi, Kenya's capital. She arrived in Nairobi, where Clo and her family were waiting for her, on April 3—Jane's 23rd birthday.

On her way to Clo's family farm, Jane got her first up-close look at an African animal: a giraffe with beautiful dark eyes and long lashes. She was amazed!

Jane spent three wonderful weeks on Clo's farm. She didn't want to leave, but it was time to start the job she'd found as a secretary in Nairobi.

Shortly into her stay, Jane's friends told her that if she wanted to study African animals, she needed to meet Dr. Louis Leakey. He was a scientist who studied **anthropology** and **paleontology**. Amazingly, Dr. Leakey's secretary had just quit, and he needed someone for the job. When he heard how much Jane knew about African animals, he hired her on the spot!

One day, Louis told Jane about a troop, or group, of chimpanzees living on the shores of a lake in Tanzania. Nobody had ever studied chimps in the wild up close before. Leakey wanted to find out more about their lives because he knew how much chimps and humans had in common. He needed someone brave to take on this important job.

JUMP IN THE THINK TANK

Some things you want to do may seem scary but are worth it in the end. What is something you've done that scared you at first but was worth facing your fears?

This project was Jane's big break! Dr. Leakey saw how patient and observant Jane was. She would have to take notes and spend hours in the **rain forest** where the chimps lived, watching their behavior. He knew that she was the right person for the job, even if she wasn't trained as a scientist. It would fulfill her life's dream, but it would also be dangerous to live in the jungle with wild animals.

Welcome to Gombe

In the 1960s, there weren't many female scientists. The main jobs available to women were: teacher, nurse, secretary, and waitress. Jane didn't care about the limits other people put on her. She wanted to study chimps.

> "Since I was eight or nine years old, I had dreamed of being in Africa and living in the bush among wild animals. Suddenly, I found I was actually living in my dream."

Government officials didn't believe it was safe for Jane to study the chimps alone. So, her mother volunteered to come along to Gombe, a game reserve in Tanzania, where Jane was to carry out her **research** on chimps. On July 16, 1960, Jane and her mom set out for Gombe.

Day in and day out, Jane watched the chimps from far away with borrowed binoculars.

Jane bravely hiked through the thick forest every day. She had to watch out for spiky vines, snakes, and flies that bite, all while looking for the chimps. Some days she would spot a few chimps, only to see them run away when they noticed her!

Jane wanted to get closer to the chimpanzees so she could better observe them, but she didn't know how yet. She was the first scientist to ever study them in the wild. Jane was excited to see how they lived, played, ate, and made friends. Deep down, she knew that humans and chimps were similar, just like Dr. Leakey thought, but could she prove it?

WHEN?

1957	Jane becomes Leakey's secretary.
1960	Jane starts working in Gombe, Tanzania.

CHAPTER 4

JANE AND THE CHIMPS

Blending In

Six weeks into her research, Jane and her mother both got very sick from a disease called **malaria**. They suffered with high fevers and chills for two weeks. Their cook, Dominic, helped nurse them back to health. When Jane was better, she started taking long hikes into the jungle again to watch the chimps. This time, the locals suggested that she take a scout named Adolf with her as a guide. They wore tan clothes as **camouflage** to blend in with their surroundings.

Jane sat in the trees and on the hilltops, looking through her binoculars and taking notes about chimp behavior. She saw the same chimps over and over and gave them names because she felt that they had their own personalities, very much like people.

From her observations, Jane knew that the chimps shared many of the same emotions as humans: anger, sadness, happiness, and jealousy. She also knew if she just watched them long enough, she could prove it.

MYTH & FACT

MYTH: Animals don't have feelings like people do.

FACT: According to research, animals feel sad when a family member dies, joy when a baby is born, and anger or jealousy when someone takes over their space.

One day, a male chimp came into Jane's camp and stole some bananas. Jane set out more bananas to attract the chimps. When a group of chimps returned to camp, they became

aggressive. They stole blankets, shirts, and pillows to chew on, not just bananas. Still, Jane wasn't scared. She cleverly set up a feeding station away from the research camp so she could observe their behavior safely.

David Greybeard and Friends

A little later on, an older chimp with a gray beard let Jane come close to him. Jane had named him David Greybeard. Jane held out a piece of fruit. When David Greybeard reached for the fruit, he rested his fingers in Jane's hand and held it. This was magical for Jane!

Another day, Jane saw that David Greybeard was holding a long

JUMP IN THE THINK TANK

Why do you think Jane's observation of David Greybeard using tools like humans was important?

grass stem and sticking it into a termite mound. He was using it as a tool to get the termites so he could eat them. This discovery was **groundbreaking**! Before Jane's observation, scientists thought that only humans made and used tools. Jane immediately sent a **telegram** about her discovery to Dr. Leakey.

She observed other chimps in David Greybeard's community. Jane used their **features** and personalities to tell them apart. Goliath was outgoing and adventurous. He was the most powerful male of the troop at that time. Flo, the oldest female of the troop, had a big nose like a bulb and ragged ears. Mr. McGregor, one of the first chimps Jane met, was often grumpy, so Jane named him after the crabby gardener in the book *The Tale of Peter Rabbit*.

Once the community of chimps trusted Jane, she was able to get much closer to observe them. She even learned how to copy their calls. In a way, Jane was speaking to wild animals just like Dr. Dolittle! Jane's dream was coming true.

But the chimps were in danger. Loggers were destroying the chimps' habitat, and **poachers** were even killing them! She knew she had to protect them. The best way to help was to keep researching and reporting on the chimps so more people around the world would care about saving their habitats.

WHEN?

In October, Jane discovers a chimp using tools.

1960

Tanzania becomes a country.

1964

CHAPTER 5

DR. JANE GOODALL

National Geographic

When news of Jane's research and discoveries reached England and the United States, scientists thought her research wasn't valid, or true, because she was a woman who had no real scientific training, and she hadn't gone to college. Still, her work caught the attention of the National Geographic Society, a famous organization that was created to explore and protect the planet. This organization decided to give Jane and Dr. Leakey money to help pay for their research. They also sent a photographer named Hugo van Lawick to take pictures and make a movie about Jane and the chimps.

At first, Jane didn't want anyone to join her. The chimps trusted Jane. She didn't want a new person scaring them off. But, when Hugo came to Gombe to take pictures of Jane with the chimps, she saw that he blended right in. Jane and Hugo became very close friends. Eventually, they fell in love and got married.

In August 1963, *National Geographic* published an article by Jane called "My Life among the Wild Chimpanzees." It featured Hugo's photos. After the article came out, scientists could no longer argue with Jane's findings. Jane and her chimps became world-famous!

University Life

As news spread of Jane's findings about the chimps, Dr. Leakey decided it was important for Jane to go to a university and get a degree in science. Since Jane had done years of work with chimps in the jungle already, Dr. Leakey was able to get her into a program for her **doctorate**, or PhD, at Cambridge University. He believed scientists would take Jane more seriously once she had a degree.

In 1962, Jane began her studies at Cambridge. Right away, her professors told her that she was doing it all wrong! They said real scientists labeled animals with numbers, not names. Still, Jane knew that animals were just like people, with different personalities and features. From growing up with her childhood dog, Rusty, she'd learned how important it was to give animals names.

Many of the other students and professors talked about how to study animals, but they had never actually worked with animals in the wild. Jane learned new things, but she also taught the other scientists about what she had observed.

While at Cambridge, Jane missed Mr. McGregor, David Greybeard, Goliath, and Flo. She couldn't wait to get back to Gombe for good!

MYTH & FACT

MYTH: Chimpanzees are monkeys.

FACT: Chimpanzees are apes. Chimps and humans are related. Our DNA, the material in our cells that makes us look and act like we do, is 98.6 percent the same as a chimp's!

In the meantime, she visited the troop of chimps whenever she could. In 1964, Flo gave birth to a baby boy named Flint.

Jane graduated with a doctorate in **ethology** in 1965. Her final paper was about wild chimpanzee behavior. She was a **primatologist**, or someone who studies primates like chimps.

Jane wrote about how chimps eat, play, fight, communicate, love, and protect one another. She explained that they are **omnivores**, which means they eat both plants and meat. She also wrote about the sleeping nests chimps make out of leaves. Jane's hard work paid off. It was official—she was now Dr. Jane Goodall!

WHEN?

1962 — Jane starts her PhD program at Cambridge.

1963 — Jane's article for *National Geographic* is published.

1964 — Jane marries Hugo. Flo gives birth to Flint.

1965 — Jane graduates with her PhD from Cambridge.

CHAPTER 6
FAMOUS JANE

Home Sweet Africa

After she graduated, Jane went back to Gombe with an even bigger dream: She wanted to open a research center. Jane asked the National Geographic Society for money to help build her center and they gave it to her! Students from all over the world came to the center to study with Jane. In 1965, Jane became even more famous after a one-hour TV program aired about her work.

Unfortunately, in 1966, some of the chimps came down with **polio**, a disease that can make it hard to walk or move. Jane knew the chimps needed help—and fast! She decided to dedicate most of her time to spreading an urgent message about the chimps' situation.

Jane's life changed in 1967 when she and Hugo had a baby boy named Hugo Eric. Everyone called him by his nickname, Grub.

Jane spent mornings working on research reports while someone else watched Grub. In the afternoons, she'd play with Grub and teach him to swim.

Jane loved being a mother, but she also missed the days when she could wander the jungle alone watching the chimps.

> "There is no doubt that my observations of the chimps helped me to be a better mother, but I found also that the experience of being myself a mother helped me better observe chimp behavior."

Change among the Chimps

In 1971, something shocking happened: A divide began to form among the chimpanzees, separating them into two groups—one in the north and one in the south. A few years later, in 1974, the group of chimps from the north began attacking lone chimps from the south. For the first time, Jane learned that chimps sometimes hurt one another. This aggressive period lasted from 1974 to 1978, and came to be called the Four-Year War.

Just before the war began, in 1972, Dr. Leakey passed away. His death motivated Jane to work even harder to help

JUMP IN THE THINK TANK

Why do you think chimps fight just like humans?

the chimps by keeping their center going strong. She traveled the world to raise money for her cause. Traveling took Jane away from her family. Hugo and Jane grew apart. The two got divorced but remained close friends and shared in raising Grub.

After the Four Year chimp war, things in Gombe changed and became too dangerous

for Jane to live and work there. Right around this time, Jane met the director of Tanzania's national parks, Derek Bryceson. They worked together to keep the research center open. They also fell in love and got married.

Soon after, Jane and Grub moved to the city of Dar es Salaam to be with Derek. Jane was no longer living in Gombe, but she didn't give up on her chimps. She founded the Jane Goodall Institute, which allowed local Tanzanian researchers to continue her important work.

WHEN?

1967 Jane gives birth to her son, Grub.

1974 The Four-Year War begins.

1975 Jane marries Derek Bryceson.

1978 The Four-Year War ends.

CHAPTER 7
THE WORLDWIDE STAGE

Saving the Chimps

Even though Jane spent less time working with the chimps in Gombe, she was still focused on saving them and their habitats. Some local people were poaching chimps. They were also cutting down the forests where chimps lived.

The number of chimps in the wild was going down. Jane chose to become an **activist**.

JUMP IN THE THINK TANK

Why do you think laws are important in protecting endangered animals?

She worked on behalf of the chimps by speaking and marching in order to get the government to protect them.

Sadly, Derek passed away from cancer in 1980. Jane was very sad and decided to go back to Gombe to spend some time watching the chimpanzees. Being there helped her begin to feel better.

In 1984, Jane founded ChimpanZoo, a program that helps make sure chimps in zoos have bigger living spaces and activities to keep them active and healthy. Two years later, in 1986, Jane published a book called *The Chimpanzees of Gombe*. This book led her to help form the Committee for Conservation and Care of Chimpanzees, or CCCC, a group that pushed for the US Endangered Species Act. There was also an international treaty called CITES that helped protect the chimps. This agreement between countries around the world protects animals from being traded illegally or unsafely. By 1990, chimps were listed as **endangered** because of their shrinking habitat. Jane was not about to let them disappear completely. The chimps were, after all, her family.

She worked with US and African government officials to add chimps to the list of protected species.

To spread the message about saving the chimps, Jane started traveling the world to speak. She spent no more than three weeks in any one place.

Jane's Work

In 1991, Jane founded another important organization, Roots & Shoots. It helps young people everywhere make a difference by showing them how to plant trees and take other steps to improve the environment. Today, there are more than 100 countries with Roots & Shoots groups. The United States alone has about 2,000 such groups. In 1994, Jane started TACARE to make sure that Tanzanians had a way to improve their environment. People involved with this program have planted more than a million trees in Africa to grow new forests for the chimps to live in.

> "It's the young people today who give me the greatest hope for the future."

Throughout her life, Dr. Jane Goodall has been not only a friend to the chimps but someone who has worked tirelessly to save them.

Without Jane's hard work, African chimps may have become extinct. Today, Jane still spends most of her time fighting for chimps and other endangered animals. She raises money for research and habitat protection through the

WHEN?

Derek dies of cancer.

1980

Jane publishes *The Chimpanzees of Gombe.*

1986

Chimps are declared endangered.

1990

Jane starts Roots & Shoots.

1991

TACARE is formed by Jane and friends.

1994

Jane Goodall Institute. She tours globally and speaks as a voice for the chimps and for all living animals, as our planet faces some dangerous changes. Jane often starts her lectures with a chimp greeting call.

Grub grew up and had a family of his own. Jane owns a house next to them in Tanzania. She tells the story of David Greybeard, Flo, Flint, and the other chimps to audiences everywhere. She hopes more people will join in the fight to protect endangered animals, including chimps. Some 60 years after her journey in Africa began, Jane continues to be a champion for chimpanzees!

CHAPTER 8

SO . . . WHO IS JANE GOODALL?

Challenge Accepted!

Now that you know so much about Jane's life and work, let's test your new knowledge in a little who, what, when, where, why, and how quiz. Feel free to look back in the text to find the answers if you need to, but try to remember first.

1 Where was Jane born?

→ A Gombe, Tanzania
→ B Paris, France
→ C London, England
→ D San Francisco, California

2 What was the name of the nature club Jane formed with her sister and two neighborhood girls?

→ A Chimpanzee Club
→ B Alligator Club
→ C Kids Club
→ D Rat Club

3 **When Jane was little, which animal did she observe laying an egg?**

→ A Hen
→ B Snake
→ C Spider
→ D Duck

4 **What was Jane's first job?**

→ A Waitress
→ B Secretary
→ C Scientist
→ D Mother

5 **How did Jane first get to Africa?**

→ A On a plane
→ B By car
→ C On a train
→ D By ship

6 **Who went to Gombe at first with Jane?**

→ A Hugo, the photographer
→ B Derek, the national parks director
→ C Vanne, her mom
→ D Judy, her sister

7 What were the names of some of Jane's chimp friends?

→ A Oscar, Big Bird, and Elmo
→ B David Greybeard, Goliath, and Flo
→ C Dora, Diego, and Boots
→ D Jubilee, Penny, and Rusty

8 Jane first rocked the scientific community when she discovered that chimps do what like humans?

→ A Have babies
→ B Eat bananas
→ C Make and use tools
→ D Fight

9 Where did Jane do most of her work with chimps?

→ A Gombe, Tanzania
→ B Dar es Salaam, Tanzania
→ C London, England
→ D Chicago, Illinois

10 Which organization did Jane form in 1991?

- → A Roots & Shoots
- → B TACARE
- → C CCCC
- → D ChimpanZoo

Answers: 1. C; 2. B; 3. A; 4. B; 5. D; 6. C; 7. B; 8. C; 9. A; 10. A

Our World

Jane's life and work changed our world. Let's look at a few things that are different because of the work Jane did, and continues to do, to this day.

- → Chimpanzees are protected as a part of the US Endangered Species Act, along with other animals that are at risk of becoming extinct. It is illegal for people to hunt many animals, including spotted owls, Mexican wolves, flying squirrels, and some types of caribou. CITES helps regulate, or control, the trade of animals around the world.
- → Programs like Roots & Shoots help kids all over the world save the environment by showing them how to plant trees and make others aware of how to protect endangered animals.
- → Zoos in many cities and countries have made the spaces where chimps live bigger and better.
- → The world is more aware of how similar humans and chimps are. Jane's discoveries led to people protecting these animals. At age 85, Jane still travels to share their story and raise money to protect them and other endangered animals.

JUMP IN THE THINK TANK FOR MORE!

Now let's think a little more about what Jane has done and how her work and courage have affected the world we currently live in.

→ How did Jane's research, and the attention she got for it, help chimps and other animals survive?

→ How does Jane's determination inspire you to push through tough times?

→ How did Jane connect with the chimps? How do you connect with animals? Are there any animals you call by name and whose personalities you know?

Glossary

activist: A person who works to bring about change for something they care very much about

aggressive: Ready or likely to attack

anthropology: The study of human beings and how they behave

camouflage: To make a person, animal, or object blend in with its surroundings

conservation: The protection of a plant, animal, or other element of nature

DNA: The material in each human, plant, or animal cell that controls how each looks and functions

doctorate: The highest degree awarded by a graduate school or college (also known as a PhD)

endangered: When something's existence is threatened

ethology: The study of how animals act, especially where they live

extinction: When a species, or type, of animal dies off

feature: Something that makes a person or animal different from others

groundbreaking: When something has never been done, seen, or made before

habitat: Where a plant, animal, or other organism lives

malaria: A dangerous disease spread by mosquitoes that causes fevers, muscle pain, tiredness, and sometimes death

naturalist: A person who studies nature

observant: When someone carefully watches or listens to something to learn about it

omnivore: An animal or person who eats both plants and meat

paleontology: The study of fossils or remains of prehistoric creatures left in rocks

poacher: Someone who hunts or captures wild animals when it is not legal to do so

polio: A disease that causes fevers; stomachache; pain in the back, arms, and legs; and sometimes leg paralysis (when you can't move your legs)

primatologists: Scientists who study primates, such as gorillas, orangutans, chimpanzees, and lemurs and work in biology, medical research, anthropology, and zoology

rain forest: A thick forest of trees with consistently heavy rainfall

research: The study of a topic in order to find new information

telegram: A message sent over an electrical wire that is delivered in written or printed form

Bibliography

Goodall, Jane. "An Evening with Dr. Jane Goodall." October 21, 2019. San Francisco.

Goodall, Jane. *In the Shadow of Man*. Rev. ed. New York: Mariner Books, 2000.

Goodall, Jane. *My Life with the Chimpanzees*. Rev. ed. New York: Aladdin Paperbacks, 2002.

Goodall, Jane, with the Jane Goodall Institute. *Jane Goodall: 50 Years at Gombe*. New York: Stewart, Tabori & Chang, 2010.

Goodall, Jane, with Phillip Berman. *Reason for Hope: A Spiritual Journey*. New York: Grand Central Publishing, 1999.

Horton, Robert. "Award-Winning Documentary Gazes Lovingly at Jane Goodall." HeraldNet, November 30, 2017.

Jane Goodall Institute. "Timeline."

Leakey Foundation. "The Four-Year War." Podcast. *Origin Stories,* November 19, 2018. Audio, 26:55.

Morgen, Brett, dir. *Jane*. Washington, DC: National Geographic Studios, Public Road Productions, 2017.

National Geographic Society. "Chimps and Their Tools." Video, 2:33.

Nicholls, Henry. "When I Met Jane Goodall, She Hugged Me Like a Chimp." *Guardian,* April 3, 2014.

O'Reilly, Katie. "A Trove of Unseen Footage Reveals Jane Goodall's Early Explorations." *Sierra Magazine,* December 15, 2017.

Wei-Haas, Maya. "New Jane Goodall Documentary Is Most Intimate Portrait Yet, Says Jane Goodall." *Smithsonian Magazine,* December 6, 2017.

Acknowledgments

First and foremost, I want to thank Jane Goodall, whom I got to see speak in San Francisco when I began the research for this book, for being such a determined advocate for animals. It was an inspiration and an honor to research and write about Dr. Jane Goodall, whose work I emulated as I set off 28 years ago, at age 20, to work in a Costa Rican rain forest. I appreciate my outstanding editor, Orli, who entrusted me with this book and guided me with grace, precision, and determination. I appreciate my parents, Janice and Ray, for their encouragement. To my brother, Steve, thanks! Kudos to my talented writers' group—Andrew, Brandi, Evan, Kyle, and Sonia. In memory of my grandma Grace, my aunt Judy, Joe McClain, and my mentor, Ilse. To my nephews, Sam, Jacob, and David; and my nieces, Sofia and Katherine. Thanks to the entire Callisto team! I am supported by family and friends: Michelle G., Susan, Ann and Greg, Danielle, Jeanne, Deborah, Kiernan, Laurie, Tanya, Carla, Julia and Ira, Maureen, Amparo, Michael, Ricardo, Alejandra, Arden, Jen, Tami, Karen, Annie, Crystal, Bryan, Jessica, Marji, Marcy, Lara, Anita and Bob, Jerry, Nena and Mel, Jami, Stacy and Rick, Michelle R., Chalmers, Violeta, Diana y Juanca, Laura, Darren, and Sylvia Boorstein.

About the Author

SUSAN B. KATZ is an award-winning bilingual author, National Board Certified Teacher, educational consultant, and keynote speaker. She taught for more than 25 years. Susan has published five books with Scholastic, Random House, and Barefoot Books. *Meditation Station,* a book about trains and mindfulness, is due out in fall 2020 from Bala Books (Shambhala). Her other titles include *ABC, Baby Me!*; *My Mama Earth* (Moonbeam Gold Award Winner for Best Picture Book and named "Top Green Toy" by Education.com); *ABC School's for Me!* (illustrated by Lynn Munsinger); and *All Year Round,* which she translated into Spanish as *Un Año Redondo,* for Scholastic. She also authored *The Story of Ruth Bader Ginsburg* and *The Story of Frida Kahlo* for Callisto Media. Susan is the executive director of ConnectingAuthors .org, a national nonprofit bringing children's book authors and illustrators into schools. Susan served as the strategic partner manager for authors at Facebook. When she's not writing, Susan enjoys traveling, salsa dancing, and spending time at the beach. You can find out more about her books and school visits at www.susankatzbooks.com.

About the Illustrator

LINDSAY DALE SCOTT is an illustrator and designer in northeast Ohio. She has done artwork for several children's books including *LEAVES : A pop up book* and *Little Vampire's Big Smile* along with tons of greeting cards for American Greetings. She loves drawing animals, birds and florals along with historical and decorative figures. She currently lives with her Pastor husband Andrew, their two dogs Toby & Violet, two bunnies Sam & Pepper and their newest addition: their daughter Nora James.